IMOGEN HOLST AT DARTINGTON

Imogen Holst
at Dartington

Editors:
PETER COX and JACK DOBBS
assisted by
Heather Williams and Nan Plummer

THE DARTINGTON PRESS

© The Dartington Press
First published 1988
ISBN 0 902386-13-1
All rights reserved
Designed by Sue Snell
for Scriveners, Devon
Typeset by Reardon Graphics
Printed by Short Run Press, Exeter, Devon

Imogen Holst was born in 1907, the only child of the composer Gustav Holst. By the outbreak of war in 1939 she was established as a busy working musician in London. She taught in schools and had been on the staff of Cecil Sharp house, the Headquarters of the English Folk Dance and Song Society.

Early in 1940 she became one of the six Music Travellers appointed by the forerunners of the Arts Council to foster amateur music-making in wartime rural England, with the whole of the South West, from Oxford to Land's End as her responsibility.

The physical strain imposed by such an enormous task was great, and so, in the summer of 1942 she accepted the invitation of Dorothy and Leonard Elmhirst to spend time at Dartington. She remained there for nine years.

After twelve recuperative months, during which she again had time for composing and also helped with the Arts Enquiry on Music, she started the courses for music students with which this booklet is chiefly concerned.

Imogen left Dartington in 1951 to pursue her own career, a year later accepting Benjamin Britten's invitation to come to Aldeburgh as his music assistant. She worked with him until 1964, when the need to concentrate on the music of her father claimed her full attention.

Over the years Imogen often returned to Dartington. In 1966, with Peter Pears, she opened the new buildings of the College's Music School. Her last visit was in August 1981, when she attended Gennadi Rozhdestvensky's classes at the Summer School of Music. She died in Aldeburgh in March 1984.

For her services to music, Imogen Holst was created a CBE in 1975, was a Fellow of the Royal College of Music, an Honorary Fellow of the Royal Academy of Music and received Honorary Doctorates from the Universities of Essex, Exeter and Leeds.

The Editors wish to thank the following for their help in the preparation of this book:

Mary Bride Nicholson: John Stanyon: Rosamund Strode: John Wellingham.

Edith O'Hanrahan and Joanna Harris for permission to use their rounds.

Published by Dartington Press with financial assistance from the Holst Foundation.

Additional Comments: Peter Cox

Imogen said much in this interview, but were she to read the transcript now there are some more things, I think, she would have liked to have recorded herself.

The close mutual friendship with Dorothy and Leonard Elmhirst and her deep respect and admiration for them was always evident and shows clearly in their personal correspondence. She shared her enthusiasms with them, was grateful for their support and always insisted on the debt she owed Dartington.

Florence Burton is not mentioned. With Winsome, Florence was one of her closest friends, not only as an ever-willing secretary and support of the students but as a teacher of ballet to scores of small girls in the district. Imogen, trained as a dancer herself, had great respect for what she was achieving and gave her constant help and encouragement.

She also says little about the great musicians she attracted to Dartington — Benjamin Britten, Peter Pears, Joan Cross, Clifford Curzon, Michael Tippett, Alfred Deller and others who came not only to perform but to take part in activities with the students, many of them much less universally recognized than they were later to become. And, of course, there was that remarkable quartet of young men, led by Norbert Brainin whom she does mention at length — who gave their first Wigmore Hall recital, I believe, at Imogen's personal expense, after a memorable public rehearsal in our own Great Hall.

There were others, too, who took part in her work, whom she greatly valued: Sybil Eaton and Marie Reckless who joined the staff as teachers of the violin; Helen Glatz, composer and

Winsome Bartlett

INTERVIEW

other great musicians who would come here. They would come for a day or two and then they would go away again. And I thought, I must not get into the habit of this. I remember walking round this exquisite garden in early Spring and thinking "now, you could live here for the rest of your life". It seemed a kind of heaven on earth, and then thinking "no, because you are a musician, and you have to go on learning and you have got to go on having really strict criticism". So I asked in the late '40's if I might leave, and it took some time to find a successor, and '51 was the year when it was possible. But it has been wonderful coming back over and over again and feeling that this is a second home and always will be.

Photo: Catharine Scudamore

Benjamin Britten

Jack Well, I can't tell you how grateful we are to you for coming back and giving us your inspiration and for all that you have done for us. Thank you very much indeed.

27

pianist; Elmslie Philip, Chief Education Officer for Devon; Cecil Cope, County Music Organiser and Nellie, his wife; Mervyn Bruxner and all the other musicians closely associated with Mary Ibberson and the Rural Music Schools Association. There was a great sense of a musical fraternity, with a shared feeling for the music and the way it was being made.

The partnership she created with Chris Martin was crucial for the future. Together they conceived the idea of creating an arts centre where music and the other arts could be a living experience for the locality, of seeing this as an appropriate background for training musicians who were going to work in villages and schools, and of Dartington also as a place which could attract the great and the good, and a wider public, for shorter periods. This was the concept which I was able to hold on to through that long, slow and arduous period of development in the 1950s which reached some sense of culmination early in the 1960s with the creation of the College, the Devon Centre and the Dartington Arts Society. Imogen's clarity of mind was to prove a constant source of stimulation and support when trying to keep the boat steady in what was often to prove a stormy sea.

Another aspect she does not mention, although it was central to her thinking: her generous wish to see the other arts develop side by side with the music, particularly literature and writing. She welcomed with open arms Dorothy Elmhirst's weekly Shakespeare class which so many students will remember with a great sense of gratitude. She also encouraged an interest in 'other' musics, going herself in her last year at Dartington to Santiniketan† and bringing back a post-graduate student, Chinchore, to work with her students, thus keeping up and helping to build Dartington's concern for international contact.

As far as I was personally concerned, Imogen was an education in herself. I had imagined that music could only flourish on a scale which allowed for symphony orchestras, choral societies and operas, only to find that Imogen, with a handful of students, could make music pervade life at the Hall in those dark days towards the end of the war. Every season, every birthday, every important arrival or departure was celebrated with a round or a fanfare, and it was always the kind of music that went to the centre of one's being, even if one was, like

† See pp. 71-73

myself, musically illiterate and destined to be one of Imogen's few musical failures.

A repertoire, too, began to develop which not only made for some lovely social occasions but also gave many of us a sense of belonging to something special.

I shall never forget the experience of listening to the performance of the *St John Passion* in the Great Hall. I had been away in the U.S.A. and had heard none of the rehearsals nor been involved in any of the preparations. For two or three minutes I thought it was all going to be embarrassing — the choir sounded thin and the first soloist uncertain. But, before I knew where I was, I was totally captivated and profoundly moved by the unfolding of the Passion, in exactly the same way as I had experienced the previous summer in seeing for the first time Giotto's frescoes in the Scrovegni Chapel in Padua.

Imogen taught me, and I am sure many others, about the presentation of music. She created a sense of space — in time as much as physically, so that even the most modest pieces and the humblest performers, could be properly heard and understood. She put performer and audience at ease by creating silence without asking for it, and at the end there was a pause, always followed by appreciative words and usually a request for a repeat.

She was often asked in my presence — what do you mind about most? Her reply was usually as follows. First, making the composition class the core of her teaching, and in this, at that time, she seemed almost unique among the musicians with whom I was associating. The second was to help students find the right source of inspiration — an emphasis not only on the 'how' i.e. the technique, but on the 'what', the music itself. In both these aspects she was completely in tune with what Clifford and Rosemary Ellis were doing for art teachers at the Bath Academy of Arts, to which Imogen was a frequent visitor.

As she indicates in her interview, some students were highly critical of her methods, and there were others who were also afraid of what seemed her 'other worldliness', often describing her as 'airy-fairy'. In fact, as so many of us were able to find out, she was incredibly down to earth and remarkably specific in her thinking and actions. Her emphasis on punctuality, on good preparation and on choosing the right music for particular people and particular occasions created an air of incisiveness which is missing in a great many educational institutions. Her belief that the musician should sing for his supper counteracted any sense of lotus-eating for which Dartington was always being, I think unfairly, criticised, and her instinct to become increasingly critical of students as they became more advanced dispelled any undue sense of conceit or complacency.

When Imogen decided to leave, we had to discuss a future without her. Her feeling was to close the courses. It had been wonderful while it lasted but it was better to start again with something new. There were many moments later on when I feared that she may have been right. But I am glad that we did not follow her advice. She left us, as both Leonard and Dorothy did in their separate ways, with a sense of purpose and direction, and a perception of standards — human and artistic — which however difficult to reach, remain fundamentally worthwhile and important.

A note on Dorothy and Leonard Elmhirst and Christopher Martin: Peter Cox

For the reader who did not have the privilege of knowing Leonard and Dorothy Elmhirst or Christopher Martin, the following notes might be of interest. It is clear from what Imogen said in her interview with Jack Dobbs that she regarded the presence, support and affection of all three as fundamental to her work at Dartington. For fuller details reference can be made to Michael Young's *The Elmhirsts of Dartington - The Creation of an Utopian Community*†.

Dorothy, daughter of William C. Whitney, was American in origin and inherited from her father a substantial fortune. She married Willard Straight whom she met in China and had three children by this marriage: Whitney, Michael and Beatrice. Willard died of influenza in Paris in 1918 and Dorothy was to meet Leonard at Cornell University, N.Y., where she was financing one of the first student union buildings in the U.S., later to be known as 'The Straight'; Leonard was on the committee as postgraduate representative.

Leonard was the second son of William Elmhirst, parson and squire of an ancient family estate near Barnsley in Yorkshire. He had hated his preparatory and public school education but had thrived at Trinity College, Cambridge. Being intended for the Church he joined the YMCA in the 1914/18 war and served in the Middle East and India where he became acutely conscious of rural poverty and to this cause he decided to devote his career. He was advised to go to Cornell to study agricultural economics as a necessary preparation. While at Cornell he not only met and

† Published Routledge and Kegan Paul. London 1982.

INTERVIEW

the hotel I heard the most beautiful violin practice I have ever heard in my life. It was just two notes, to and fro, very slowly, very beautifully played, and I just stood there with my ear to the keyhole. Well, later on I heard the Church performance and was introduced to Norbert, and I thought this is a real violinist.

Now, soon after that, when we got our students and Sylvia Bor, she said, "I think you should ask Norbert to stay a few days here at Dartington". He was having a very

The Amadeus Quartet. Martin Lovett, Siegmund Nissel, Norbert Brainin, Peter Schidlof.

hard time when he was out of work and was having difficulty really in finding the next meal. She said, "He is very fond of food, ask him here". So we asked him and straight away he began playing with our sixteen year old students. They weren't all sixteen year olds, but some of them were very young. Norbert just stood there on that spot of the Music Studio leading them and helping them, and I sat on the floor, as it might be there, watching him and seeing how he helped them with everything. And his relaxation before coming in and that extraordinary power of continuity of the rhythm going through — I learned so much which has helped me ever afterwards when I have tried to conduct. And also I was so moved to find it happening with these young elementary students because it is so rare to get a very great player with such gifts. We talked for a bit and I asked him what he was going to do now that the war was over. Was he going back to Vienna? He said, "No, I think the centre of music in the future will be in England".

I think it was on the visit after that (because he came back several times) he said, "Imo, I would like to start a string quartet". He had already got his great friend, Peter Schidlof, who, as I expect you know, had so generously given up the chance of a career as a solo violinist in order to play viola in the quartet. He had got his great friend Siegmund Nissel, and he had just found this new young cellist, Martin Lovett, who hadn't been a refugee but who had the same kind of playing. I said, "Yes, Norbert, that is a marvellous idea, come and give a concert here in Dartington". And he said, "Yes, we will begin rehearsing". And we talked about programmes and we then got this series of concerts in memory of Christopher Martin. We had a summer festival of concerts in the Great Hall and Peter Cox and Dorothy welcomed the idea. Now, where else would you get people saying "Yes, let them give a concert in six or eight weeks time", when the quartet hadn't even begun to be put together? But that was the sort of thing that happened, they took my word for it that this would be something terrific. So they came and gave their first concert in the Great Hall. And after that they would come on visits and play with us informally. It's been a wonderful link.

Jack Very exciting. Then in 1951 you decided to leave?
Imo Well, I decided to leave before then because I knew that I couldn't go on with that sort of life for too long. This will be awful for people who hear me saying this, but I will say it, as if future strangers aren't in existence, and I will say it to you who are my friend. But you will realise that when one is always teaching amateurs and future professionals who are still immature, one needs constantly to be criticized on one's own music by someone who one knows is a better musician than oneself. Now, in South Devon, we had so many blessings but we hadn't many musicians better than me at that time. We had visitors, wonderful visitors who would come into our lives — Benjamin Britten and Peter Pears giving recitals, the Amadeus and

been so important. When you got together you always made music. You sang rounds together. There was music on all occasions, and this must have made the whole place alive in the most remarkable way.

Imo It was lovely. A day I will never forget — the day war was over in Europe. It was a summer day and of course all work stopped and we had very few students then, only about eight or nine. We went up the tower and sang Boyce's *Alleluia* and *Glory be to God on High* rounds, with the sound going round the courtyard. That was lovely. And then another thing I will never forget. When Dorothy and Leonard had their 25th wedding aniversary Ruth†commissioned Benjamin Britten to write some part songs. He chose (I think Ruth must have suggested it, knowing how both Dorothy and Leonard loved the garden here) *Flower Songs*. And we went on Leonard's birthday — now that is in June isn't it? — on to the bit of lawn behind the private house and sang them for the first time. We couldn't manage all of them but we sang three of those *Flower Songs* with Leonard at his study window there and the windows open. And to be able to do that sort of thing — great music, commissioned for great people such as Leonard and Dorothy — and to have their own students singing it on their own lawn. That was a lovely feeling.

Jack Very exciting. In a strange way it links up with Santiniketan‡ where, when the rains come, all the students celebrate and dance and sing. Let me ask one other thing — what about the Amadeus Quartet? They were associated in their early days with Dartington.?

Imo Now, that was owing to our cello teacher, Sylvia Bor. I'd heard this wonderful young violinist, Norbert Brainin, in the days of Hans Oppenheim*. You know that Hans Oppenheim took his more professional group to Cambridge? I went to one of his concerts there, and he had Norbert Brainin playing in a small orchestra for the Bach Cantata they were doing in a church concert. Norbert was staying in the Blue Boar Hotel in Trinity Street and I had to go in with a message. As I walked along the corridor of

---

† Ruth Elmhirst (Ash) daughter of Dorothy and Leonard Elmhirst
‡ University in West Bengal founded by Rabindranath Tagore
* Director of Dartington Hall Music Group 1937-1944

INTERVIEW

expects in a school or a community nowadays where people are making music together, and yet many students are not getting these things even now.

Imo No, I think it is this old thing that we complain so bitterly about — bureaucracy and all that. It's stupid to go on complaining about exam syllabuses in an art, but we know how difficult it is to get exam questions which will tell the examiner this is a superb teacher in the making. It will always be like that.

Jack It is the difference of actually removing the communication between people, and instead trying to get it on paper, whereas your students were involved the whole time with human relationships, with people as well as with music activities.

Imo But you see, they couldn't go on. People have said to me, "Why didn't it go on like that?" and it is the old, old thing that when it begins to grow it can't go on. When it began to grow we wanted a larger staff. We therefore needed money, we therefore needed not to go on asking for Dartington money — they started us off, but we needed government money, we needed Ministry grants, we needed Local Education Authority grants. Therefore we needed a syllabus that the inspectors would approve of, and we needed these exams with the marks so that the students could be recommended when they left here to get a teaching job. I forget how many students there were, only about twenty-eight or thirty when I left. To me that seemed a lot to be carrying on in this free way of doing all the things we did being joined up together.

Jack Nevertheless, I still think it is an ideal one ought to hold on to.

Imo Oh, so do I.

Jack Even if one does go into a certain traditional situation or pattern, one must never lose this central thread.

Imo And you still have Dartington.

Jack Oh, exactly, very much so, and after all why shouldn't some of these students be HMI's themselves, and break down some of these barriers we are talking about?

Imo Jack! What an idea. Oh! That has made my day. That is absolutely wonderful.

Jack Well, talking about 'making days', could we perhaps finish on the whole matter of celebrations which seem to have

Two rounds by William Boyce in Imogen's manuscript and taken from 'A book of rounds for Leonard and Dorothy, Christmas 1942'.

well and have realised that they did learn in spite of us being so unorthodox.

Jack When you say 'out of work' what does that mean? Does that mean that they couldn't find the right employment to satisfy themselves?

Imo But, dear Jack, you get students who are out of work as soon as they have left, don't you? Do they all go into jobs?

Jack No, they don't all go straight into jobs, but on the whole they can get jobs if they really want to. I was wondering what it was that made them be out of work.

Imo Well, to begin with, if you are keen on composition more than anything else you are not likely to get a job as a composer. I used to tell them when they were learning composition here (I'm not talking about the Estate workers but real composition pupils) that of course it was wonderful for them to be able to hear their things being tried out on the orchestra or by a good soprano. We had, for instance, Noelle Barker as a singer here who was lovely at singing the new songs that had been written just the week before. No, I tried to tell these composition pupils while they were still here that composition isn't a subject one can expect to earn one's living at straight away. I told them how my father, when he left college, had to earn his living as a trombone player, and even Benjamin Britten had to begin writing music for films when he left college.

Jack I just wondered if it was because they were given such freedom they couldn't find their place in a rather tight traditional system?

Imo No, because I am sure you will agree with me that the freedom that Leonard and Dorothy and Chris Martin, and later Peter Cox, gave us here to do the music we wanted to do in the way we wanted to do it — that freedom, if properly used, gives more discipline through the actual use of it than any other way. When you give up being a student and go out into the world to earn your living, it's the discipline of the musician that counts whatever your job is.

Jack But apart from that, with which I agree entirely, the whole of the training they were having, with all this variety of activities was so practical — so essentially practical — for the jobs they were going to have. I am thinking of the things you were talking about just now — exactly what one dashed at full speed across this room and knocked his copy to the floor and carried on. He saw the point and heard where he was from either side of him, picked up his copy and went on. That was the sort of way we worked.

Jack You must have been exhausted after this?

Imo No. It was very hard work, but it was all my own choice and I was absolutely spared from what is a nightmare to me at this moment, the responsibility of a certain amount of organisation which I have with the Aldeburgh Festival and the future of Snape Maltings. Life then did not consist of one committee meeting after another as it had done in C.E.M.A. jobs, and also this problem of discussing where the money was to come from. That was all right, and my only worries were musical ones. When it is one's job and one is allowed to choose the music one wants to do, those worries are not worries — they are part of living. The exhaustion at the end of the day is not desperate exhaustion but is really the exhilaration at the end of a lovely day of lovely music.

Jack There must have been a tremendous sense of satisfaction seeing all the parts working together, rather than having compartments and different systems.

Imo When you say satisfaction, I don't think one is ever satisfied on the artistic standard side, but also it is quite right that these young students should have been dissatisfied with a great deal that went on at Dartington. When people talk about student unrest these days, well, I had quite a bit of unrest. I can remember several students who really were most dissatisfied with the way we did things. They would have been happier if it had been not so free and if things had been in compartments, just as you are saying it must have been nice that they weren't. They would have found it easier, if we had had grading exams and all that. I can remember on one or two occasions when students left they would write to me quite bitter letters complaining that I hadn't taught them properly and that therefore they were out of work. And of course I, thinking back to my own student days and remembering what it felt like to be out of work coming back from a travelling scholarship, knew it was part of being young so I swallowed hard and didn't mind the beastly letters. Since then these two students I am thinking of have done very

Imo Oh, yes, but that was towards the end of my time. I think that was almost my last performance, I can't quite remember chronologically†. No, it wasn't — we did the *B Minor Mass* after that. We took three years to rehearse the *B Minor Mass*, and people were astonished at that and thought it would get stale but we had the chance that could only have happened in Dartington. For instance, we had our violin technique class, bowing and fingering the difficult bits in the B Minor. We also had the young solo singers among the students having singing lessons on their solos. We had, of course, the choir divided up into the main chorus and then the semi-chorus of our own students doing the difficult bits in between. We had harmony at the keyboard working out all the figured bass. We also had what I hate teaching as a subject and never have, the subject of musical analysis. My father never taught musical analysis, so I never did it as a subject, but we went right through the *B Minor Mass* living every note and finding the most extraordinary links with keys. For instance whenever Bach went into Eb it would be the Incarnation, and the message coming down from Heaven and that would link up with some quite different chorus or solo when the Eb phrase came in again — the modulation — absolutely fascinating — and the musical form; the links too, with the speed and the foundation in the dance. Of course I had this passion of doing music through dance, which was one of the reasons why it was lovely having Winsome here.

We didn't only do Bach and Handel. We were even wild enough to do the Verdi *Requiem* with piano and with all our own soloists. Rosamund Strode was then our leading soprano and she sang it most beautifully. Now, we sat round at rehearsals in a big semi-circle and Leonard was one of the best tenors. Of course he went wrong every now and then, and I remember at our final rehearsal I saw, to my horror, Leonard prepared to come in after several bars rest with a very important tenor lead — a bar too soon. I knew that he would bring all the other tenors in and it would break down, so, from where I was conducting I

† L'Allegro — March 1947. St. John Passion — March 1948. Mass in B Minor — July 1950.

19

thing was to get accepted by the Ministry. I wonder if it would be very rash if I told you that one of the inspectors who came to listen to a composition class sat next to me on the sofa while it was going on and said "What textbook of improvisation do you use here?". Can you imagine? A different inspector — a rather higher up one — came on the day that Sylvia Bor was going to play her cornet, and of course everyone got hysterics — just everybody. But it didn't matter because we got accepted, which astonished a lot of our students.

You see, some of them couldn't believe that the way I taught them was going to get them through exams. They didn't mean to be rude, but the look of absolute astonishment on their faces when they came back at the beginning of a new term and said, "But Imo, I've passed my exams, I've got ARCM". Absolute astonishment, but it did help them, and it helped in an extraordinary way. For instance, this business of the rural orchestra when you play an instrument that you don't know. You learn how long it takes to get your instrument ready when you've had it down, and the conductor has been saying, "when you get there, you must do that better and that better — now let's go from letter C". You have to find letter C and then you have to pick up the instrument and pick up your bow and find the first note and look at the beat. It takes an awfully long time. Well, unless you have experienced that, you go out into schools with a lot of elementary school children around you and you say, "letter C" and wonder why they are not ready. Those things really did help enormously.

Now we also had one of our evenings open to the Estate — Friday evening was singing evening. There had always been a tradition of singing on the Estate and I was asked to carry that on. We did Bach Cantatas and we did Handel's *L'Allegro*, a shortened version, in the Great Hall. That was lovely. We had quite a large choir and I remember particularly one of our best basses was Mr Tucker, the police constable from Totnes who has died, alas. I don't think I ever heard such beautiful amateur singing, with perfect Bach phrases. I can just hear it in my mind.

Jack Was that the group that performed Bach's *St. John Passion?*

the staff. We were going to hear a recital by a great pianist. There we were in the audience and there was the piano, when someone found to their dismay that the pedal was squeaking and there was no piano tuner available. I said, "It's all right, I have a couple of students here and they know how to do it". In front of the audience, with the great pianist waiting in the wings, our two Dartington students crawled under the piano and put the squeak right.

Winsome not only repaired all the strings but she also began the experimental making of recorders. Unfortunately that didn't go as far as it should have done, chiefly because we asked her to do too much. I was keen that we should have musical handwriting classes because even now professional musicians can't write music. You can't read what they have written, and there is a great waste of time.

In the days that I was here we didn't have exams. Anyone who wanted to go in for an exam could do so. My only two compulsory classes were musical handwriting (which Winsome took) and musical dictation. When they got good enough at either of those they could give it up.

Of course, we sang. We sightsang unaccompanied every morning — Palestrina, di Lasso, Vittoria — from 9am to 9.30am but nobody dreamed of calling that compulsory, because it was such a joy.

Now, this business of arranging everything took a lot of time but it all leads up to teaching students how to arrange music. One of the things we had in this studio was a rural orchestra amongst the students but with no outsiders. Each week one student would be in charge as a conductor, having arranged and written out the music. We would sit around with an instrument in our hands that we didn't know how to play — the noise was horrendous. I remember how our distinguished cello teacher, Sylvia Bor, had decided she would like to play the cornet and the sounds she made! Well, it would happen, but the Tuesday composition class which was going to render something with a cornet part for Sylvia was on the day we had our first inspector, our first HMI.

Jack You had an HMI?

Imo Oh, we had to have a series of HMI's because we couldn't go on for ever on Dartington money, and then the whole she retired. She played violin and viola here. We had April Cantelo as one of our singers and she played the viola very well in the orchestra. I can remember when we were still in this studio and rather elementary, the extraordinary sounds going on behind her head and, without stopping, she turned round to see what it was, while still going on playing.

Now, I want to link up this orchestra, which then got so big, with the fact that Winsome, among all the other things she was doing, taught us instrument repairs. When anything went wrong, all the string players went up to Winsome's workshop. She not only did the repairs, but held classes in how to do instrumental repairs. Also, we had Mr Harris of Harris Osborne† come in and teach the elements of piano tuning and repair. People sometimes said to me, "But you can't expect amateurs to do anything when a piano goes wrong". Now, let me tell you what happened in the second Summer School of Music, which, in the late '40's was at Bryanston, not at Dartington. Some of my students were able to go for a week while I was on

Imogen with William Glock, founder of the Summer School of Music, at Bryanston 1949. The Summer School has taken place at Dartington since 1953.

† Piano firm in Paignton.

INTERVIEW

have been there as an audience.

Jack Can I ask about the orchestra, because presumably it wasn't the kind of orchestra one thinks of in formal terms?

Imo No! We had at one time something like seventeen descant recorders, all out of tune, very shrill; hardly any of the players could read notes, but of course the orchestra helped them to do so. You must have the picture of a row of percussion, some of them quite small children, some of them Estate workers who simply couldn't read a note of music but were given a tambourine, and every time I smiled at them they played the tambourine. Then we had Leonard Elmhirst playing the cello. Did you know he was a cellist?

Jack Oh yes, indeed and he said he chose your prettiest student to teach him, if I remember rightly.

Imo Well, he may have said the prettiest, but later on when we got more students we had wonderful cello teachers, absolutely wonderful — Sylvia Bor and Pamela Hind — but before they came he played in a very elementary fashion in the enormous orchestra of sixty in the Great Hall, and sitting half a yard from him was Dorothy playing guitar. Now did you know that?

Jack No I didn't.

Imo Of course you can imagine the worries that Dorothy had in the war, not only the personal worries of her family, but also the responsibilities of all those extra people, the school children and everything going on around this courtyard — and we found that the happiest look on her face during the week was when she came out of her house swinging her guitar on her way to this studio to play with the orchestra. She was awfully good because she was very musical — she really was — but unlike Leonard she was shy of going on being rather elementary.

To return to the orchestra. We had one of our original students, the boy, playing trumpet. He had always wanted to play the trumpet, so he played the trumpet and that was rather loud. We had a sprinkling of strings, and later on we got some good strings because they were connected with the Rural Music School. I give you the impression that we were all dumb but that was in the very old days! Later on, after a few years, we had Muriel Anthony who, as you know was Director of the Kent Rural Music School before

Winsome was so marvellous. By then I had grabbed her on to the staff. She was working in welfare on the Estate, doing the interesting war work which Laban† pioneered — you know that he had the job of inventing movements, chiefly for factory workers, so that they didn't get tired? Well, Winsome had become highly trained in that and was teaching people in the sawmills. I quite immorally stole her away from her work there and said I must have her in the Arts Department.

Jack The Music Training School was in the Arts Department?

Imo It was never grand enough to call it that. You couldn't, with six or seven students at the age of sixteen call yourself a Music Training School with capital letters. It acquired a name later on when we had government help and approval. The wonderful thing when I started was that Chris, Leonard and Dorothy didn't care two hoots what I did and I had an absolutely free hand. That was how I was able to have Winsome doing so many things to help us. You know how desperately tired pianists get? Well, Winsome used to bully them and make them relax. She used to make the singers stand up properly, she used to make everyone move properly. One of the things I started when we got a few more students was a class called 'presentation'. They had to come on with whatever their instrument was. If it was the piano, they would come on to applause, then they would bow and smile and then they would sit down, but they didn't actually have to play. They would then get up, we would applaud them and they would bow and would have to walk off the other way. Now you know the agony of self-consciousness — you become absolutely rigid with fear and nerves, and Winsome's exercises helped there.

Jack We have a person on our staff today who insists on this 'presentation' very strongly and he would appreciate all you are saying. Students can be very tense, very shy and very embarrassed, and presentation involves knowing how to move well.

Imo And also the feeling of graciousness, to look grateful for the fact that people have come to hear you play or sing and

---

† Rudolf von Laban, inventor of 'Labanotation' — a system for recording movement. Laban stayed at Dartington from 1938-40.

forget when they came to our composition class. Also we had a lot of people from the Estate — those who hadn't gone off to the war. In the early days of Dartington they had become used to having a lot of amateur music making and so they welcomed it. We had political refugees. One of my lovely composition pupils who had never done a note of music was the distinguished ex-Colonel Federico de la Iglesia from the Spanish War. He had been on the losing side and had had to come with his family to England. He taught languages in Foxhole School, and I can still see his smile when four music students sang the round he had made up in the composition class.

We had an orchestra open to anyone. We began in this studio but after a time it wasn't large enough and so we went into the Great Hall. At one time we were sixty strong but hardly any of us could play. I remember — I don't think she would mind if I mention her name, as she is such an old friend — Marjorie Fogden, who played second violin. I used to have her, as she hadn't done much music, just under me, as it were, when I was conducting. She played with another second violin who, again, was rather elementary. Every now and then one or the other of them would get out in their bowing arm, so I would see Marjorie doing an up bow and her partner doing a down bow. I would be horrified that they were going to hit each other.

Another thing I remember when we were still in this room. It was Christmas, and we did one of my father's easy carol arrangements for voices in unison and ad lib orchestra. The cellos weren't all that good. There was a teacher from Foxhole (not a music teacher, I forget what her subject was), she was very keen but she didn't know an awful lot. She was all right when she climbed up from the open string, but unfortunately in one of the carols she had to plunge to a low Eb on the C string and the sounds that she and her partner made were one of the few things that defeated me. I had to stop and get the giggles because it sounded just like a prehistoric sea monster. However bad we were, we went on. I had to arrange most of the music, and, to begin with, I had to write out the parts myself. Then, as we got more students it became part of their training as future Rural Music School teachers to learn how to arrange and write the parts out. That was where had been working in the early days before it was taken over by the Government, through the Rural Music Schools with my friend Mary Ibberson whom I already knew and admired so much.

I suggested to Chris, and later to Leonard and Dorothy, that this would be a golden opportunity to train young music students to be future Rural Music School teachers, but we didn't want to limit it to that. I had learnt from my father before I learned it from anyone else, that you don't want to have either just Rural Music School teachers or just brilliant young singers or violinists. In such a community as Dartington there was a wonderful chance to mix them all up together and let them learn from each other. And that was Chris Martin's idea. Of course, it was war time and to get students they had to be sixteen years old and no older, because of conscription. So we started in September 1943 in this room, the Music Studio†, where all the classes happened as long as I was here. We started with four sixteen year olds, one boy and three girls. Two of the girls had come from the local school in Totnes. Oh! we had a part time older student who did some teaching of music in Foxhole, so then we were five. We were very ambitious — we did Benjamin Britten's *Ceremony of Carols* before it was published. Right from the beginning we had open evenings of music every night of the week during our term for anyone who was living at Dartington or round about who would like to come.

Now, you won't realise, Jack, what 'anyone' meant. We had land girls, very keen they were, and they used to come in apologising for not having had time to remove the mud off their clothes. We had evacuee school teachers, because Leonard and Dorothy gave up nearly the whole of their house, as you know, to young school children. The children couldn't come because they had to go to bed by that time, but their teachers came, and of course were thrilled because they had come from London and were used to having things happening in the evenings. Later on, when America came into the war, we had wounded American airmen who were convalescing here. That was another of Dorothy's wonderful ideas, and I will never

† Studio in Courtyard, now called the 'Ship Studio'.

that Leonard Elmhirst† had been so pleased about some rude remarks I had made about church singing. I had said that people in church services quite often sang so badly that it was only the Almighty that would have put up with it. To my horror I found that he had written to the Archbishop telling him about this.

Anyway, that was the way I began working in Dartington and one day, as I was crossing the courtyard, I got a message that Chris would like to see me in his office. That is the office which is now the front room of the Devon Centre. He said, "Imo, how can we start at Dartington the sort of thing that your father did in the old days in Morley College?" Well, Morley College nowadays has a very high standard of music education, with its three orchestras, its opera and conducting classes; but when my father started in 1905, before I was born, it was really amateur. He achieved a great deal because he cared passionately about lovely music being done by anyone who wanted to do it, whether they were good at music or not, as long as they were keen and turned up regularly every week for rehearsals. So they did Purcell's 'King Arthur' and Purcell's 'Fairy Queen' and Bach Cantatas with people who could hardly play at all. That was the tradition in which I was brought up.

The other thing that I would like to mention he did at Morley College in those days (because it does link up with Dartington) — he started a composition class every week for grown-up beginners, some of whom didn't know their notes. They could hear a tune in their minds but had never thought how to write it down. They were that elementary, and were of all ages — some retired, some still working as tram drivers, office workers or school teachers. That impressed me a lot. So, when my father died in 1934, I thought, if ever I had the chance to carry on that tradition I would do so because no one else was doing that. Teachers were beginning to think about composition in schools: now it is a matter of course. But when Chris Martin said "How can we start at Dartington?" I thought, what a wonderful opportunity! It linked up with the work for C.E.M.A. I had been doing with amateurs, because we

† Dorothy & Leonard Elmhirst, Founders of present day Dartington 1925.

These principles and ideals remain central to the present music courses at Dartington, where students continue to be encouraged to realise their musical potential to the fullest possible extent, and, at the same time, to explore ways of using their abilities and understandings with a variety of people and in many different communities.

Imo We have been listening to my friend Winsome, playing one of my very favourite country dance tunes.
This interview was preceded by a recording of Winsome Bartlett playing the country dance tune 'Nonesuch' on her pipe and tabor. (Ed)
Jack Winsome came from a country dance background, didn't she?
Imo Country and Morris, the English Folk Dance Society, that's where we were friends for many years.
Jack She was at Dartington when you arrived?
Imo No, I arrived at Dartington before I worked here. I came to Dartington when it was part of my C.E.M.A. Music Traveller's region. That was in the war, when what is now the Arts Council began and I was given seven counties in the South West to work in, mostly with amateurs. Devon was one of the counties, so I came down and had marvellous nights here. You can imagine what a joy it was in the war.
Jack Living at the Hall?
Imo Yes, spending the night here and then going on working round my seven counties; but the job was really impossible in those days because we were told to spread it as far as we could throughout England, and yet conditions were so difficult: there was no petrol for transport. I used to have to walk from one choir practice to another which could be five miles, and I am afraid I did get over weary. I was encouraged to give up that particular job after two years, and, as this had been in my region, I came to Dartington for a few days to have a holiday. While I was here, Chris Martin† asked me if I would work on the Arts Enquiry‡. That was marvellous, because I had been around in this side of England and I was able to do a bit. I remembered

† Christopher Martin, First Administrator of the Arts Centre at Dartington Hall 1934-44. See p.36
‡ The Arts Enquiry. Music: A Report on Musical Life in England. Sponsored by the Dartington Hall Trustees. Published P.E.P. 1949.

Introduction: Peter Cox

Imogen must speak first. It is her voice we all want to hear most. Those of us who have written about her are only too glad to take second place. Following this introduction is a transcript of an interview, held in the Ship Studio, between herself and Jack Dobbs, recorded on video in 1976 and played eight years later on the occasion of a reunion of staff and students at Dartington to celebrate her life.

Those who knew Imogen will be able to hear her voice coming through, the inflexions, the pauses and those moments of heightened expression culminating in a guffaw or slap of her hand on her knee. In the interests of brevity and ease of reading, I have taken the liberty of doing some minor editing, but always with that sense of dread of Imogen's reaction to documents I used to ask her to read; her criticisms could be devastating.

Many of her students, some now in distant parts of the world, have contributed to this booklet. Selections have had to be made from their writings to avoid too much duplication of content, but the entire collection will be kept in the Dartington archives. Each contribution was striking in the freshness of the forty year old recollections and each showed how lasting has been the impact of their years at Dartington. All acknowledged the lifelong debt owed to Imo's inspiration and training. The students have carried into their work as Instrumental and School Teachers, County Music Advisers, Professors at Colleges of Music, Directors of Rural Music Schools, Professional Players or Singers, Composers, Musicologists, Administrators of Music, the high principles and musical ideals that were kindled and fostered by Imogen.

Contents

Introduction: Peter Cox, followed by transcript of interview with Imogen Holst and Jack Dobbs	9
Additional Comments: Peter Cox	30
A Note on Dorothy and Leonard Elmhirst and Christopher Martin: Peter Cox	34
Imogen and her teaching: Extracted from contributions by her former students: Muriel Anthony: Edward Bor: Margot Bor: Kay Burdess: James Butt: Jack Philip Cannon: Joan Crispin (Pendered): Ann Crittall (de Lisle Burns): Luke Gertler: Joanna Harris: Bridget Headley (Jones): Gerald McDonald: Ania Michaelis (Lentz): Grisell Roy (Davies): Gabrielle Rosenberg (Foti): Gay Sclater-Booth (Seth Smith): Elgin Strub (Ronayne) Mary Lou Williams (Potter): Heather Williams: Elizabeth Winship (Streatfield)	39
The early years of the Music Course, remembered by the first students	46
Further recollections of Imogen's teaching Contributions from:	51
Pamela Hind (O'Malley)	53
April Cantelo	54
Georges Fueter	56
Sara Starling (Doniach)	56
Noelle Barker	57
Ania Michaelis (Lentz)	59
Etain Kabraji (Todds)	60
John Wellingham	61
Rosamund Strode	64
The rehearsing and performance of Bach's *Mass in B Minor*	68
Imogen as student-teacher in India: Jack Dobbs	71

fell in love with Dorothy but was summoned to New York by Rabindranath Tagore who invited him out to India to set up a programme of rural reconstruction for the villages surrounding his family ashram at Santiniketan in West Bengal which, with its pioneer school and arts institutions, had just become the International University of Visva Bharati. Dorothy encouraged him to go and provided the money that enabled the work to get under way.

Dorothy and Leonard Elmhirst and their daughter Ruth. May 1947.

They married in 1925 in the U.S.A. and bought Dartington Hall the same year. Much of the organizational structure which evolved derived from Leonard's experience with Tagore. Much of the inspiration for the development of the educational and arts programmes came from Dorothy and her contacts in the U.S.. Dorothy's own particular interest was in the theatre.

Up to his retirement in 1972 Leonard was constantly in and out of Dartington — Chairman of the Trust, intensely interested in forestry and agriculture and also in the various building programmes. He was a great supporter of individuals, particularly of craftsmen and women on the estate, and always the first to recover — and help others to recover — from disappointments and mistakes. He had an essential 'up-beat' and enthusiasm which was extraordinarily encouraging to those of us who worked there. Meanwhile, he was one of the founders of P.E.P. (Political and Economic Planning) in London, Founder President of the International Conference of Agricultural Economists, which took him all over the world, a constant visitor to India as an adviser to the Government before and after Independence; later he developed a close association with Tanzania.

It was Dorothy's almost constant presence at Dartington which helped to hold things together and provide an atmosphere that was humane, caring and sensitive but at the same time demanding and adventurous. She was extremely knowledgeable as to what went on and who might be in trouble. She attended innumerable occasions and performances, sat in on rehearsals and was an acute critic. Everyone wanted to know — sometimes with great anxiety — what she thought; a congratulatory letter was something to treasure. Without Dorothy's constant support the arts programme would never have been sustained through all its difficulties; she was delighted when the College of Arts was eventually brought into being. She died on December 14th 1968 on the very day when her last public gift — the Theatre School at Dartington — was finished.

Christopher Martin was appointed Arts Administrator at Dartington in 1934 with a difficult brief; to bring some administrative and financial order into the various arts activities going on at the Hall and at the same time to make preparations for the induction of the Jooss-Leeder School of Dance and the Ballet Jooss itself which the Elmhirsts had already invited, and the Chekhov Studio which came to Dartington through Beatrice Straight†.

Curiously enough Chris had had a previous association with Dartington. His grandfather had been Vicar at Dartington for many years, the family being connected by marriage with the Champernownes who had owned Dartington for some 350 years; his uncle Jack was now Vicar and his uncle Keble, later to become famous for his flower paintings, was Vicar of a nearby parish. As a boy on holiday Chris used to bicycle through the roofless Great Hall.

† Actress daughter of Dorothy Elmhirst by her first marriage.

However it was through a connection of his wife, Cicely, that he was invited back to Dartington. Her family was connected with McKenna & Co whose senior partner, F. A. S. Gwatkin, was Dorothy's lawyer and a Dartington Trustee. Chris had been President of the O.U.D.S. at Oxford and on leaving had gone to work in the City. This mixture of experience in the arts and business was to prove invaluable in what was probably the first arts administrator job in this country. He did a wonderful job, very much alive himself and greatly supportive of the artists he had to administer; he became a great personal friend of the Elmhirsts. Sadly, he was dogged by persistent ill-health and died in 1944. Henry Moore's 'Reclining Figure' on the top terrace of the tiltyard was commissioned by Dorothy as a memorial to him.

Photo: Kate Mount

Photo: Brian Heseltine

Madrigals in the Gardens and the Courtyard.

Imogen and her Teaching

I look back on my two years at Dartington and my association with Imogen as having been the greatest of all influences on my musical life. The magical combination of the place and the personality had most of us spellbound and reluctant to come down to earth when our time was up. I was sixteen when I arrived, straight from boarding school and probably at the most impressionable time of life. Imo was the first to ignore that I was the baby of the class and I was grateful for that. I was given things to do that I was convinced were quite beyond me, but my howls of protest were met with raised eyebrows, a slight smile and a nodding head, and I found myself being practically hypnotised into composing, arranging and playing anything she asked for.   *E.S.*

I suppose it is true that in a life spent in one's chosen profession only a handful of people will influence one really decisively by the strength of their personality. I am sure it was far from Imo's mind to wish to exert such an influence on the people surrounding her, but it was unavoidable.   *E.B.*

Her speaking voice was clear, articulate and wonderfully expressive. She would linger over a certain word or syllable to give it emphasis — "Isn't it ma-a-a-arvellous?". She was able to produce a beautifully constructed sentence, every word carefully chosen to express what she meant. She had a way of making anything interesting, even if it was basically dull, and she had the ability to put over an idea in the most logical way.   *L.G.*

It was part of Imogen's genius that she could inspire you to surpass yourself. *E.S.*

Imo! What a privilege to have known her and even more to have been one of her students at Dartington. No one before or since has ever revealed to me so much about music. Her own innate musicianship and her facility for passing on her ideas with such clarity that even the dullest student could not fail to follow the thread was an inspiration. *M.A.*

Imo was a most gifted composer as I learnt when she wrote a short opera *Benedick and Beatrice*† to words from Shakespeare's *Much Ado about Nothing*. It was performed in the Barn Theatre as a double bill with James Butt's opera *Noah*. The part of Don Pedro was to be sung by Cecil Cope, but he could not be available for all the rehearsals. Imo asked me to be his understudy and coached me with the part. I was no singer but I enjoyed these sessions. She was forever giving me encouragement and praise. Whenever I got something right she would say "That was ma-a-a-arvellous. Let's do it again". The music was so beautifully written for the voice that I never found the part difficult. On the contrary, the feeling and expression was all in the music. All one had to do was to sing; the rest came automatically. *L.G.*

What, on her part, was thoroughly worked out beforehand appeared spontaneous in performance. *E.B.*

I had never met anyone like her before — she danced about in her muted cotton skirt and blouse, woolly cardigan, woven shoulder bag, with her sandy hair drawn tightly back in a small knob, her pale face animated with her humorous eyes. I was completely captured by her unique, charismatic personality and it was the beginning of a love which all of us had for her ever after. *M.L.W.*

She had a memorable way of expressing herself. Once while she was playing a Mozart Trio with my mother and myself, we were not getting the speed of an Allegretto right. Imo turned on the

† Performed 21.7.51.

piano stool and said "Let's think of this movement as a middle-aged Allegretto" — and all was well.   G.R.

Looking back through a lifetime of professional experience, I think the most important thing she did for me was to cement in me those high creative ideals, combined with practical common sense, which she inherited directly from her father. She was constantly quoting things Holst used to do and say which inspired me at a tender age with musical compositional values which have formed the bedrock principles of all my writing.
J.P.C.

Imo conducting with dance-like movements, the whole of her body conveying the music. Sometimes she just stood still for a moment, listening and gazing upwards, a finger on her lips. And in the short silence at the end of a rehearsal or concert, she would beam at us, slightly nodding her head, and we all felt her saying "Well done".   G.R.

Under her flexible conducting, singing early Baroque contrapuntal music was a very special musical experience. The music always seemed to emanate from her very being, so well had she absorbed it and become part of it. What of it that she was teased about her ballet-dancing feet on these occasions? That was all part of it and typically Imogen.   K.B.

In general, however, I remember most vividly her avid wish to learn herself from everyone she taught and from everything she did. This is the hall-mark of all great teachers; they maintain an artistic alertness based upon a constant inner enthusiasm, coupled with a consciousness of relativity and proportion.
G.McD.

Imo had a delightful sense of humour. She would laugh heartily at a joke or comic situation, her whole being enjoying it to the full. Yet, when telling a funny story herself, she would do so keeping a straight face. I remember once when she was taking us for madrigal singing, there occurred the word 'kissing'. She stopped and said "This reminds me of an occasion when I was

taking this very madrigal† with a group of students some years ago. One of the students asked 'Excuse me, Imo, do we breathe before or after kissing?' ''. She remained quite serious while we all collapsed with laughter. She waited for us to quieten down, and, without another word, continued with the rehearsal.
                                                                L.G.

After a bit I got used to doing apparently impossible things at a moment's notice.   A.M.

Just as Imo danced when conducting because her whole body was involved — so her personality stamped itself on our lives. Imo opened windows in our lives which nothing and nobody can ever shut.   M.L.W.

In Imo's life there was no time for anything but bare bones and those bones had better be good! I, who am an inveterate clutter collector, often think with envy of Imo's room at Dartington. There was nothing, but nothing visible in it, and yet it didn't look bare — just pared down to essentials. I suppose that is why, although I have worked and studied under many other musicians, it is Imo's face that I see so often when in doubt about some musical matter. Living, as I do 8000 miles away in Western Canada, in a part of the world where musical discrimination is yet in its infancy, I spend a lot of time going through possible choir music, trying to sift the wheat from the chaff and at the same time to come up with something acceptable to the circumstances and the era. If uncertain, if I am wondering whether in all conscience this is music that I can accept, so often I see Imo looking over my shoulder. If her face has that rather solemn look I know that it has to go quickly into the waste basket, it is not genuine and if pared down to the bare bones it would disappear. But if her eyes are dancing then I know I can go ahead and do it and enjoy it, even if it isn't out of the top drawer — because of its kind it is genuine and the structure is good.   B.H.

I don't think Imogen ever wasted a moment of time while teaching, in what was, I suspect, a highly organised personal life.

† Fair Phyllis I saw sitting all alone: John Farmer

She seemed to be absorbed in music with an almost religious single mindedness but was also full of life and fun and enjoyment of the good things of life. I remember her remarking that music in England would be better if we had more appreciation of good food and wine.   G.R.

There was no dilly-dallying either if one found oneself walking with her — perhaps to one of the local schools. It was difficult even for those of us with longer legs to keep up with her. This constant urge forward — from our point of view — seemed inherent in all she did. With this pressure, and her deep sensibility, she suffered greatly at times from the controversy she inevitably met about her methods. Perhaps she ranked individual musical and spiritual qualities more highly than is often done; perhaps in those delectable surroundings in the country she felt impatient with the routine of the more 'normal' examination work. But perhaps her students gleaned something very special and unobtainable elsewhere — never to be forgotten memories of her idealism and inspiration.   K.B.

Imo had that wonderful quality of turning every event into a happening.   E.B.

I remember an occasion when two students were playing Arthur Benjamin's *Jamaican Rumba* on the two grand pianos in the large studio. Imo, who happened to be present, was suddenly inspired by the lively rhythm of the piece. She removed her cardigan, flung it on to a chair and began to perform a marvellous and spontaneous dance.   L.G.

What stands out for me is no one particular occasion but Imogen's personality and the quality of the music of all kinds which she was able to produce with us. Imogen moulded the varied group together using each person's individual abilities and bringing out the best in them to make music which came up to her high standards. She always made rehearsals interesting and rewarding in themselves and, while insisting on accuracy, good intonation and rhythm, and on listening to what we were doing, she had a gift for making quite ordinary people appreciate and enjoy the process of 'learning the notes' as much a part of the musical experience as the final performance. Her marvellous sense of rhythm and pace and the enjoyment of the music which she conveyed, always made her conducting most exciting.

G.R.

Imogen and I met for the first time outside the shop-window of Boosey and Hawkes, the music publishers. Imogen looked small, rather pale, with fair hair dressed in ballerina style and she wore a brown tweed suit. Any immediate impression of frailty or weakness was broken, however, as soon as she spoke; we introduced ourselves and began to talk of various matters and, when she began to describe the community of music students at Dartington, I began to realise that here was a very strong, vital and generous personality indeed. We really had a number of practical matters to talk about, but I seem to remember that they rapidly disappeared into the background as the subject of music took our conversation over. I showed her a number of compositions, and these included the austere *Variations for Piano and Strings* which I'd completed under Seiber. Imogen's incandescent enthusiasm and lively energy with which she did all things, were something quite new to me; perhaps because she had many qualities which were really quite unique — and I was grateful for her complete honesty when she looked at the score of the *Variations* and said, "You know, I really find it a little difficult to hear this in my mind's ear; if you come to Dartington I think we should perform this, it will give the string students something meaty to work on and at the same time you'll have a chance to see whether this piece 'comes off' ". *J.B.*

I first met Imo when she interviewed me as a prospective student for Dartington. It was a very informal affair; she had a wonderful way of making one feel at ease. There was little response after I had played my cello piece, which she accompanied herself on the piano, but when I came to play my Haydn Piano sonata, her reaction was quite different. She began to conduct the music and sing along with it, ending with "Isn't it ma-a-a-arvellous music?". I've wondered since whether it was Haydn that really got me into Dartington. *L.G.*

Students who had never written anything before found that they could compose, timorous players blossomed into confident performers. Her unique combination of demanding and achieving the highest standards coupled with attention to practical details such as writing special parts for players with limited ability, made her training an ideal one for those of us who went on to work in Rural Music Schools. *M.A.*

Rhythm always seemed to me to be the essence of Dartington. It was there that I learned that rhythm was not just a natural gift but something for which you also had to strive. I suppose Winsome had a lot to do with that — and Sybil Eaton — and certainly John Wellingham, that folk dancer par excellence. But over it was the presiding spirit of Imo whose every movement and gesture was the embodiment of rhythm. How well do I remember one thrilling occasion when we danced *Jack's Maggot* with Imo accompanying at the piano. I suppose I have been struggling ever since to try and achieve, with my numerous choirs, just that kind of phrasing and movement. *B.H.*

The time at Dartington with Imo was a wonderful period of hard work, friendship, laughter and enjoyment of Music, Art and Nature. Her pupils are eternally grateful to her for all she taught, not only about music but about life itself. *J.H.*

The early years of the Music Course remembered by the first students

The people that were at Dartington during the first two or three years of the Music Course were privileged to have more of Imo's teaching and her company than was possible later on when numbers grew and more staff were appointed. We were like a family, working and playing together. We worked hard, but we also enjoyed life and had time for expeditions to Ashburton in the 'Ashburton Flyer' from Staverton and over to the moors. I remember once six of us walked from Dartington through the lanes to Dean Prior, with Imo striding ahead and urging us to 'bend at the knees' as we struggled uphill. The little concerts we gave in various churches around Dartington were models of planning and careful preparation. We were never allowed to perform anything that was too difficult for us to do well. Even the simplest piece we thoroughly rehearsed, with careful attention to tempo, dynamics and presentation — lessons which lasted throughout my career in music.   *J.H.*

There was music everywhere at Dartington.   *M.L.W.*

At 9.15 each morning we had part singing and learned many madrigals. In 1944 we went to Cambridge on three different occasions to give wartime concerts to school children in King's College. The trains were all blacked out and we had long journeys to avoid going by London with so much bombing there. Before our early morning singing we all gargled with T.C.P. which Imo provided and insisted we used in wintertime.
     J.C.

We sang on every possible occasion — on top of the tower on V.E. day, in sunny corners of the Courtyard on a Spring day, whilst queueing for lunch in the White Hart, farewell serenades at 8am to departing guests catching the early train to London. Everyone, including Imo, enjoyed the meals — wonderfully varied in spite of rationing. Imo relished the mugs of hot soup as we queued for our main course and the delicious hot coffee for breakfast. When the first strawberries and cream arrived after the war, she announced that she would lick the plate, and she did, standing up for all to see! *J.H.*

Students and staff on music studio steps 1945

It is hard to imagine how different life would have been in these last forty years without the influence of Imogen's style — not only in music but in her interest in craft. Her friendship with Winsome was a sharing of these interests; they liked woven fabrics and furnishings, choosing with flair and confidence of colour and design.

Imo's devotion to and support for Florence was also an example to us, based as it was on her admiration for Florence as a person, as an efficient personal secretary and as an enthusiastic teacher of ballet to young children.

We have a collective view of Imogen's friendship and also each one of us a very personal one. I always felt when, in later years, she came to stay that she took me out of a case, like a trombone, gave me a polish then back I went into the box!

We all have treasured memories and occasions that were highlights. For me, the most simple and moving one was singing from the top of the tower on V.E. Day, followed by country dancing with Winsome. Navy days were exciting and for us an innovation, as suddenly there were 40 or so extra players with our small group. We saw then the expert way in which Imo handled larger works and resources and were impressed with her skill in arranging parts. A letter in the archives written by a former Naval man after hearing a broadcast of Imogen's, proves that the days were remembered by some of them too, even after forty years.

Britten's *Ceremony of Carols* left a lasting impression because of the tremendous attention to detail during preparation of the work, followed by the excitement and atmosphere of the performance. A private disaster happened when I fell backwards from the highly polished bench and the large wrought iron candlestick swayed and splashed wax from the twelve candles over us. Imo, unperturbed, went on conducting in her heron-like way!
H.W.

Our two years at Dartington were sheer joy. Imo taught us almost everything — piano, recorder, orchestral playing, singing, conducting, choral singing. She introduced us to Bach Cantatas and chorales, Purcell, Monteverdi, Vittoria as well as folk music, folk dancing and we learned to try composing, and arranging for orchestras and choirs. Imo had no use for academic music — it was to be experienced and tried. This philosophy was passed on to me and has been the single radical idea which I have tried to carry on into my musical life — that music is an experience of the whole body and mind.
M.L.W.

I am sure I learned the love of music in its deepest sense, but her love of life also — the things that made her laugh, her wonderful ability to listen to very amateur efforts and still give serious and constructive help, and her completely clear attitude to life and everyone she met. No falseness anywhere. *A.C.*

THE EARLY YEARS

I spent two of my happiest years at Dartington from 1943-1945. Mary, Esther, Gordon and I were the four original Rural Music School students, having just left school — and the war was still on. My knowledge of music was very limited, but with Imo's help and inspiration I soon enjoyed piano lessons, accompanying, sight singing, recorder and even a few violin lessons with Robert Masters, a member of the Dartington Piano Quartet who was then living at a rather isolated farmhouse near Gara Bridge. This journey took all day. We took a packed lunch and caught a train from Totnes to Brent, then on the Kingsbridge line to Gara Bridge. We walked a few miles to the farmhouse, had our lessons plus a scrumptious cream tea before we repeated our journey back to the Hall in time for supper.

Marjorie Fogden gave us a few typing lessons and we took it in turn to be Imo's secretary each week. We typed her letters and made phone calls. *J.C.*

A student comment on the climate!

ST JOHN REHEARSALS THIS WEEK.

Monday 11-12 Recits. Gerald + IH
4.30-6 All singers and players (except Gerald and Margot)
[We have a few. If there let this man go. If this man were not a malefactor, let us then not send it.]

Tuesday. 11-12 Recits. Gerald, Ian, Margot, IH
12-1 All strings — (1st chorus + bits that need extra practice)
4.30-6 All singers and players (except Gerald + Margot)

Wed. 10-10.45 String quartet for Haste ti Golgotha. (Muriel, Janet, Anne, Pam; also Margot)
(also sometimes Elisabeth + two Margarets)
11-12 Recits. Gerald, Pam, Margot, IH.
12-1 Es ist vollbracht. Margaret, Pam, Margot (1st Maurice to advise on ornaments)
3-4 Recits Gerald, Cecil, Walter, Pam, Margot, IH.
4.30-6 All singers + players except Muriel, Gerald + Margot. (1st chorus, and last chorus)

Thursday. 10-10.45 Sopranos + altos: Sectional rehearsals under Elisabeth and Margaret.
11-12 Recits. Gerald, Pam, Margot, IH.
4.30-5 Bass aria with choral:— Pam, Margot and all singers (also Man with cello) except Gerald.

Friday. 11-12 Recits Gerald, Pam, Margot, IH.
12-1 All strings, for Whatever needs it most.
4.30-6. Continuity:— starts and joins for EVERYONE.
[This won't involve much singing and playing, but it will be going on the same difficult jobs until they are safe.]

A detailed rehearsal schedule

Further recollections of Imogen's teaching

My piano lessons with her were often inspiring, sometimes frustrating and always on her terms. The music she didn't like, I didn't learn. This included above all Chopin and anything specifically pianistic†. It was probably a good thing as she was not able to help with technical problems, so I learnt Bach and Buxtehude, Scarlatti and Mozart. Schubert was also allowed and rather surprisingly the Schumann *G Minor Sonata* and a Brahms Intermezzo or two. The lessons resembled a conductor rehearsing an orchestra — I was told how it should sound, but how I went about trying to achieve it was entirely my business. *E.S.*

... she played a heavenly slow movement of a Haydn Sonata. Every time I hear her I am struck afresh by the loss of her as a pianist. *M.B.*

Knuckles were of great importance — they must be flexible in order to sink into chords with a really singing tone. We practised flexing our knuckles at a table often at meal times — sitting with our fingers spread out, the palms of our hands moving rhythmically up and down like spiders hypnotizing their prey.
G.S.B.

Imo's lectures were prepared and presented as if to an audience in the Festival Hall rather than to a handful of students
M.A.

† See page 54 (Ed)

Her lectures, delivered without apparent notes, were profound, full of information, timed in length to the half minute and listened to with rapt attention. *K.B.*

... a wonderful talk on Classics and Romantics that became an inspired excursion into thought and feeling.
...a marvellous talk by Imo on relaxation as applied to technique, with ballet examples. *M.B.*

... those unforgettable morning lectures! They started on the stroke of 11 and ended on the stroke of 12. There were no pencilled notes to refresh her memory, yet no hesitations, the whole was marvellously constructed and delivered with that amazing combination of knowledge and wisdom, humour and drama that only she could achieve. Each one was an inspired lesson on how to be profound in terms of the utmost simplicity.
B.H.

To me, one of Imogen's greatest gifts was her ability to create an atmosphere in which people who had, perhaps, never before tried to compose were able to express themselves naturally and creatively at however elementary a level. At the weekly composition evenings, the simplest offerings were taken seriously and appreciated. Only sentimentality and pretentiousness were unacceptable. *G.R.*

Every student was expected to compose and certainly everyone did their best. Music was naturally normally written for the particular instrumentalists available among the students and staff. Imogen's very presence was an inspiration, and her speed of perception, her ability to recognize even a spark of talent was so immediate that everyone anxiously watched her face in an endeavour to divine her reaction to the original music she heard for the first time performed at the composition class. *K.B.*

Those who couldn't write symphonies could always produce a round. One Tuesday I had written a round to a limerick of Edward Lear. The effect in performance turned out to be unintentionally funny because the third phrase was a rising minor scale and the words 'Died of despair' stood out as the other parts were still at that moment. This struck Imo as terribly funny and she laughed as I had never seen her laugh. She was in hysterics, almost rolling about on the floor and having to catch her breath. *L.G.*

Imo's teaching was 'different'. For composition it was "try it out at composition evenings". One got a pretty good idea as to whether or not one's piece was any good from Imo's "mm's", "Ah's" or nods of the head, as well as from the response of those one had persuaded to play or sing one's magnum opus. Later Imo would make helpful suggestions as to why the piece did not work, or for improving it. Counterpoint lessons were always exciting. We explored Gregorian chants, and, after Imo had been to India, compared the roots of Eastern and Western music, which was fascinating. *G.S.B.*

Imogen's course at Dartington and her way of teaching were so impressive that I found myself staying on as her colleague for nearly five years instead of the single year I had foreseen. I recall in particular the weekly composition class. Works written by the students would, after careful rehearsal, be performed, commented on by Imogen and then discussed by all. The result was a living musical concern that reached into every part of the course. Her lectures were equally live; original, perfectly documented, surprising, beautifully coherent and given without a single note or hesitation.

She loved good food, good wine, good conversation, long solitary walks. But her devotion to music was complete and within music Bach was supreme. No one was ever more sure of her values. To protect herself in pursuing her chosen work she was willing to seem odd, harsh, less than human. She was severely practical. Her status as a musician did not prevent her from attending to the smallest details, down to the exact placing of a chair at rehearsal or performance. She knew just how long she wanted the gaps between movements to be, and taught the importance of 'living through' rests. All such considerations contributed to the re-creation of a musical work. Always it was the living music that mattered. That anyone so ethereal and so full of grace in her movements could, at the same time, be so immensely scholarly was a constant source of wonder. One was made aware, through her understanding, of the natural fusion of the emotional, intellectual and physical ingredients of a work. When I asked her which of the Preludes and Fugues was her favourite, she replied, "The one I am working on." Tempi and rhythmic links in Bach were so important to her that one could almost suppose they determined her friendships. Occasionally the Friday evening singers, some of them marvellously unprofessional, would be rewarded for their efforts by Imo's delighted remark, "J.S.B. himself walked in".

My own debt to her is immeasurable; though I have been fortunate in my teachers, I owe most of all to Imogen. She had the talent of hearing afresh at every lesson with a pupil music that she already knew profoundly. Occasionally she would ask to be excused from giving a piano lesson on Chopin. It was supposed that she must dislike his music, but, as she later admitted, the reason was very different. Her disability with her left arm† had put an end to her playing of such music, and there were times when she knew she could not bear the grief of engaging, as teacher, in music that had once meant so much to her as a player. Her ideas on technique, whether given individually or in Piano Technique classes were always helpful. Her ideas on touch were exceptional; she showed that the actual intonation of the piano could be altered by the correct balancing of chords.

As teacher, writer, conductor, composer, she was outstanding. She had one more special mission — to further the appreciation of her father's music. She collected, catalogued, arranged and, where necessary, completed her father's works with selfless devotion. No composer can ever have received more loving care from a close relative than did Gustav Holst.

P.O'M.

I was certainly at a very impressionable age when I first met Imo. I had been working, in an apprentice capacity, with the Dartington Hall Music Group in Cambridge, under the directorship of Hans Oppenheim, and had been taken by the Oppenheims down to Dartington to meet the Elmhirsts, and Imo herself.

I had heard what a wonderful person and musician she was; that she was Gustav Holst's daughter ("Who was Gustav

---

† Severe phlebitis

Holst?" said I, — silently of course — not wishing to display my seventeen year old ignorance), and a composer in her own right. Anyway, there she was, hair drawn back into a little bun, feet in the fifth position, woven bag hanging from her shoulder, and for some reason shaking her head from side to side, uttering sounds something like, "Ai, Ai, Ai" as she greeted and hugged 'Oppie' and Cissy Oppenheim. For a moment I wasn't sure at all! Would I have to react to this strange bird call and submit to hugs? But no, all was absolutely all right! Quite formal How d'you do's, combined with some flattering remarks beginning "I've heard so much about..." made me feel not only at ease, but important. And it was this skill of Imo's, of making people feel important, that was one of her great teaching qualities, and which, looking back again at those student days from what I know to be older, and I hope wiser, eyes, I have come to appreciate as the first of her many teaching strengths.

When I joined the Arts Department Course, Imo became for me, and for many of the younger students particularly, the strongest influence in our lives. As a student I depended on her entirely, I admired her, had indeed been conditioned to do so, but she was an astonishing lady! She taught me piano to ARCM performance standard and she was a phenomenal piano teacher. She kept us all busy, interested, enthusiastic, and always 'making music' — writing it, rehearsing it, listening to it, and continually dealing with its practical requirements. That was the second strength in her teaching skills — that 'music', if attended to properly, with the right mixture of zest and fastidious attention, *was* a complete existence. Imo never spread such a gospel; indeed she was, surprisingly, very down to earth about normal human needs, physical or emotional — but for herself, I think music had become her life. Sometimes after a concert given by loved and admired artists, Imo was 'away', and no contact was possible. Thinking about it now, I am reminded of Isaak Walton's description of the lark who 'quits the earth, and sings as she ascends higher into the air, and having ended her heavenly employment, grows then mute and sad to think she must descend to the dull earth, which she would not touch but for necessity'. Imo had herself grown 'mute and sad' after her 'heavenly employment', and I fear that whilst we surrounded and adored her, we must have been that 'necessity'; small wonder that she delayed her return to 'dull earth'!

How tired she must have been at the end of a term — how much insistence, patience and sheer inspiration she had given out! May those of her students who now teach be as generous and selfless with *our* energies! A.C.

Whenever I think of Imo, my mind seems to keep focusing on the word 'bounce'. Obviously, a single word can never embrace the whole of a personality: it only suggests a direction, offers a little clue. The bounce for me is intimately associated with the idea of dance, of 'anti-gravity', of transmitting the joy of music-making and consequently of living. The increasing rarity of this quality, shared by Imo and our dear Winsome, plays without doubt an important part in the mental association of Imo with bounce.

Dance and Imo were one. In her gestures or poses her ballet training shone through almost continuously; also in her conducting, even probably to the point of irritating some professionals, who didn't, like us, have the privilege to know her personally. Her arms always seemed to be 'heaven-bound', avoiding, as much as ever possible, downbeats. I don't think she minded much about the tip-toeing, original sin in any conductor course!

Musically all this 'anti-gravity' led to a quite remarkable freshness and liveliness, culminating in a memorable *B Minor Mass* in the Great Hall, with clarinets instead of trumpets to avoid any 'earth-boundness'. Certainly this B Minor had more 'bounce' than any performance I have heard or played in since, but at the same time it had an unsurpassed depth and quality of emotion: that indeed was the whole of Imo. G.F.

It was all arranged — I was going to the Guildhall to study with Kinloch Anderson — but somehow I found that someone had arranged for me to go to Dartington. (This someone turned out to be Sybil Eaton, who was probably responsible for changing many lives in this wonderful way.)

First, however, an interview with Imogen had to happen. I got off the train in Totnes and the taxi climbed slowly up the hill to the Hall. It was so beautiful that I thought I'd died and gone to heaven! There was only one problem — the INTERVIEW. I was sixteen and had never had such a thing before and I was very nervous.

The taxi stopped and a magic person came dancing towards me. I remember she wore strange little soft shoes and I liked her hands, which were very flexible, and a sort of light golden brown — as was everything else about her, hair, clothes, everything — except her eyes, which were very blue. I asked her where I could find Miss Holst (I was from a polite girls' school) and she told me that she was Imogen Holst and that people called her Imo. I think we had lunch together in the Dining Hall and then we went for a walk all around the gardens, to admire the spring flowers and the leaves all coming out.

Imo talked, and asked me things, and we found ourselves at her studio. She suggested I play something on her piano and asked what pieces I knew. It dawned on me that this was the interview, and I asked if I could play something by Chopin. Imo danced around a little and said how about some Mozart. Well, at that point I was very in love with Mozart, but my school piano teacher refused to let me learn any because, as she said, my fingers were too fat. Apparently Imo did not think this a problem. I had half-learned a Mozart Concerto (K488) on my own and she gave me a lesson on it then and there, conducting and singing as I played, explaining how to play the piano from my back — which was like a reservoir of water, which ran down through my fingers into the piano. There were, no doubt, many other illuminating hints in that lesson and in future lessons. One thing that sticks in my mind about Imo's teaching is how she danced with her arms, her whole body, to get concepts across. In the *B Minor Mass* for instance, in the Crucifixus, where the music goes down and down and down, Imo would do exactly that until it seemed she would disappear through the floor.

After this first lesson (interview?), I floated out of her studio, transformed briefly from a clumsy teenager who broke everything she touched into someone a little more mature, more thoughtful — and a better musician. It didn't last long, of course, but once I started regular lessons something similar would happen each week, and gradually I began to think about music, and piano playing and even life in general in a completely different way.   *S.S.*

If you had asked me when I was a student at Dartington what I was learning from Imo I might have said "How to look at music from the inside out". If you asked me twenty years later what she had taught me I would have said "How to be a professional musician and still remain in love with music". But if you ask me the same question today my answer is unhesitatingly "By her own example, how to be a teacher.".

She taught me so much without my ever realising I was learning anything. The relationship between us was not one that I would have recognised as teacher-pupil. Quite a contrast with schooling which had been Scottish repressive, and with University where I had learned more from talking into the small hours with contemporaries than I did from scribbling down notes in lectures.

Although I held Imogen in great awe, when we worked together on songs or talked together of music, she treated me as an equal. She had no intellectual self-importance, and her knowledge had been so honestly acquired and so rigorously questioned that she could express an idea in the simplest terms. I was never afraid of asking what might seem a silly question because she would always listen, patiently consider, and positively enjoy the search for an answer which I could understand.

She had a wonderful command of English and I can still hear that precise diction and her warm musical voice. She laughed readily but never at you, always with you.

Her diagnosis of a student's level of ability and capacity for learning was like that of an experienced surgeon deciding on treatment. We all came from such diverse musical backgrounds and our ages spanned from seventeen to late thirties, but she kept us all enthralled and managed to get each of us to participate in everything. I remember so clearly the brilliant young violinist who could barely find middle C on the piano picking out 'God Save the King' with one finger, and the recent B.Mus. being asked to play it in four part harmony in the key of C♯ Major. She taught at different levels within the same framework, and praise and criticism were meted out according to each one's strengths and weaknesses. She set high standards, but the heights varied enormously from one student to another.

From every one of us there was an unspoken requirement to stretch ourselves. No shoddy work, rather leave it undone. Above all, work with a total belief in the value of what you were doing. She quoted her father's "Don't learn anything until the not knowing of it has become a positive nuisance", although sometimes, in the wilder moments of "Rural Orchestra", we also remembered his other dictum, "If a thing's worth doing it's worth doing badly".

But that sums Imo up — opposites. The formidable intellect married to an immensely practical musician. An administrator of genius, leaving no detail forgotten. As ready to show you how to put up a music stand without trapping your fingers as to discuss the finer points of some ornamentation. Fierce and quick to explode if some injustice was done either to man or music, but equally ready to burst into a wonderful peal of laughter when something amused her. Quick to debunk some facile statement, slow to demolish an idea, however absurd or fallacious, which was the fruit of painstaking thought.

Above all, she reached out to people of all sorts and made me realise that the struggling amateur is often worthy of more respect than the successful professional. She remains the measuring stick of my musical life and the invisible guide for my daily work. *N.B.*

Hans Oppenheim was an old friend of my parents. When the end of my schooldays came into view and I didn't have any clear idea what I wanted to do, he suggested Dartington. Arrangements were made and from March 31st to April 5th I went with my mother on a 'preview' visit, complete with violins and viola so that we joined in, whenever possible. For a girl of not quite sixteen, brought up in a very sheltered environment during the war, and day girl at a girls' Public School, this was a revelation. I have never been a good letter writer or diarist, but I did keep a diary of those crucial days and it makes fascinating reading after forty years!

March 31st: Arrived Totnes about 5pm, taxi up to Dartington Hall. Imogen met us. Supper in the White Hart, sat with Imogen. Community singing in the Great Hall. Students accompanied without music. Students sang spring carols in porch afterwards.

April 1st: ...to studio for unaccompanied singing, madrigals and glees. To studio at 8, heard Monteverdi records and Britten's *Serenade for Tenor, Horn and Strings*. Discussion in common-room about Britten.

April 2nd: Singing again at 9.45. Played violin in Purcell Suite with everyone playing and Imogen conducting. Tea on wall by East Wing. 5.30pm started on spring serenade following singers round estate. Ducks at Junior School objected to Winsome's

pipe and drum and looked very funny. 8pm listened to *Ceremony of Carols* by Britten on records. Played viola in quartets...
April 3rd: 10.00am sight reading singing. Did Holst's *Ave Maria* in eight parts — lovely. Played second violin in Bach chorale with orchestra under Imogen. Went to East Wing about 8pm to find out if there would be any playing. A & B took me to a film show — Deanna Durbin in 'Three Smart Girls' with Imogen's uncle, Ernest Cossart†, as Binns the butler. Very amusing, lots of love scenes. Came out roaring with laughter.
April 4th: Singing at 9.45am. *Brandenburg 5th* rehearsal at 10.15. Gala supper at long table with cider... collected signatures... guessed impersonations... skit on cello and horn recital, playing 'God save the King'; listened on lawn to singing in Hall porch at 11.15.. to bed after 12.
April 5th: ...saw Imogen waving to us last of all.
April 6th: Felt completely dazed at home after Dartington. Cannot think of world outside Dartington at all.   A.M.

I was not a music student; I didn't play or sing well, but, largely thanks to Imogen, music became my chief pleasure. My diaries for 1945-47 (when I was working quite hard for my Higher Certificate and Cambridge Entrance exams at Foxhole) record evening after evening spent at the Hall, guided by Imogen, absorbing music. She gave talks on Piano Technique, troubadour songs, listening to modern music. She introduced weekly gramophone recitals — the first impact of those Nadia Boulanger Monteverdi records is still fresh. She gave live concerts with her students, or provided us with a succession of grand visitors — Britten, Pears, Marie Korchinska, Michael Tippett — who came so frequently that they seemed to form part of a special Dartington musical pantheon. Above all she got a wide range of ordinary people, from sixteen year old schoolgirls like me to staid accountants and secretaries, to listen, play and sing. As soon as I had had my second cello lesson at school (with Sylvia Bor) I was playing open strings in Imo's orchestra, feeling a delightfully essential part of a Haydn Symphony. On May 3rd 1945, the day we heard on the wireless that Berlin had fallen, and that Hitler had committed suicide, my other great recorded excitement was being promoted to proper 2nd cello part written for Leonard Elmhirst and me, all, I

† The stage name of Gustav Holst's brother Emil

expect, comfortably in the 1st position — though I remember Leonard whispering in some agitation "Where's Bb?" My mother, Dodi, and Dorothy Elmhirst, both novices at the guitar, also had special orchestral parts composed for them by Imo. It only later dawned on me how unusual it was for a distinguished musician to take such infinite trouble over the most complete beginners.

In those years it seemed that almost every evening provided a formative musical experience, often recognised as such at the time, but cumulative in effect. Even as I sat on the floor in Imo's studio listening to Peter Pears and Benjamin Britten giving a very early performance of *Les Illuminations*, I found myself merging the beautiful lamp-lit room, the passionate, exciting new music and the sense of high occasion into a Proustian 'petite-madeleine'-like whole, a memory I knew I would revisit again and again. Imogen was often hilarious. I remember when Britten conducted what must have been the second performance of his *St. Nicolas* in the Great Hall, the pickled boys (rather uncertain little choristers from Paignton) were stuffed in the chimney at the back, where the percussion section, with its extra panoply of whips, wood blocks and gongs, prevented them from seeing Britten's beat. So, behind the backs of the orchestra, just the three of them were treated to Imo's elaborately balletic conducting — all tip-toes and ecstasy — and were utterly dumbfounded.   *E.K.*

In March 1987 John Wellingham talked with Peter Cox about his life of music, and particularly about his time at Dartington with Imogen. The following extract is taken from their conversation on that occasion. *(Ed)*

I was involved in a lot of music as a child. I started the piano at an early stage and did some dancing. I was a boy soprano, taking part in many things at our Methodist Chapel. I was taught the organ by the choirmaster-organist, and at the age of thirteen had my own organist job. I did quite a lot of music at school, as far as one could, but the problem was what to do when I left school. Someone said I had better go to see my Music Adviser, Mervyn Bruxner, in Maidstone. I sang to him, played a Beethoven piano sonata, sang and accompanied myself; and he said "I think the place for you is at Dartington". So he made arrangements for me to go down and have an interview with Imogen Holst.

At the interview I think I did much the same sort of thing as I did for Mervyn. Imogen said "Do come", and as I was free I came soon after that, towards the end of the Spring Term when Imogen was preparing for the *St. John Passion*. That was fine. I think she was short of a tenor, so she was jolly glad to have me. To come and be involved in Bach's music, suddenly like that, made me realize that was the kind of music I really wanted to be involved in, and I think that was the beginning of my early music 'nuttage' — or whatever the expression is. It was an active kind of involvement. It wasn't just being in the choir and being told what to do by the conductor. Imogen was thinking through the music, and we were sharing her involvement. We learnt how she thought that the time relationship between every movement should be thought out, so the rhythmic connection and all the pauses were very carefully controlled. When there were problems we all consulted the Bach Gesellschaft volume, and when there were continuo or other rehearsals we went to those and just sat and listened to what was going on, and learnt from that. One had read about Bach having students staying in his house who would be involved in writing out the cantata parts or preparing the singers, and I imagine that this was the way Bach went about it. For me it was very, very special.

In all we did Imogen took what we gave and built on that rather than dictated from outside. I came as a recorder player, and she got me involved with helping other students, and that meant finding and arranging music for them. We learnt by doing. She gave the impression of being airy-fairy and remote, but in fact she was intensely practical, and it mattered that people had enough music stands, that there were enough manuscript parts and that they were suitable for the individual players, that the chairs were out in the right place and so on. She minded about such things, and all these practical things have come out now in my own Centre for Organ and Early Music at Buckfastleigh. It was that kind of influence as well as the musical one, of course, that has been with me all the time.

When I came to Dartington I was a very young eighteen year old, just passionately involved in music, and so thrilled to be allowed to do what I wanted to do in it. I found it very hard to understand Imogen's feeling about the organ, because I minded passionately about the organ, and now I met a person of her standing who didn't mind about it as much as I did — and that was very hard to take. I was determined that a little chamber organ

I'd acquired was going to be used in Imo's performance of Benjamin Britten's *St Nicolas*, because there was an organ part in it, and although my organ was small and couldn't be used for driving the congregation hymns, it could be used to accompany the choir boys. Imo could easily have re-written parts for strings, but she had to put up with my determination that this was going to happen and I was going to play, particularly as Ben was coming to conduct. I remember the rehearsals — terrifying being conducted by Ben, but it was very, very exciting. I remember, too, how Imo explained that in St. Nicolas it was as if we were all sitting around the fire, and all telling a story — the legend of St. Nicolas. That created a wonderful atmosphere.

Really getting to know such a work through building up and involvement from the beginning was even more important than the performance — although when that came, we all knew exactly what we had to do; how to hold our copies, when to turn over and when not to turn over. The performance was then taken as seriously as everything else.

Imo always involved us in what she was feeling passionate about, and we caught that passion from her. And she trusted us. I was desperate to conduct the Buckfastleigh amateur orchestra so I put myself forward and we talked seriously about what I should do and how I would do it; but having done that, she trusted me to get on with it. That was the orchestra in which Winsome played, so everything was reported back, I'm sure.

Imogen's influence has remained with me ever since those days. As an organist and as a music teacher helping amateurs to make music, I have remembered the attitudes Imogen had towards helping people — the highest standards, the best possible music, and then, if necessary, adapting it, adjusting it, but without violating the core of the music.

In the following contribution Rosamund Strode recalls the shocks she received in her first week at Dartington when Imogen introduced her to her timetable and the various jobs on it, all designed to turn her into a 'useful, practical musician'. *(Ed)*

Imogen and I sat in her room on the first floor of the Barton, overlooking the courtyard, while she went remorselessly through the list in her hand, day by day, allowing no protestations or cries of alarm, until she had got to the end. It went something like this: 'On Monday at 10 you will take a very elementary harmony class in the Blue Room, and start a children's violin class at the Adult Education Centre after tea. On Tuesday afternoons there will be a W.I. choir at Berry Pomeroy; you can use the Arts Department car (this was then a solid pre-war Morris Minor belonging to Mrs Holst, and on loan for the time being) and the office will tell you about the petrol coupons. Wednesday is orchestra night; I want you to supervise, now, the addition of extra rehearsal numbers to all the instrumental parts of the Haydn Symphony we'll be playing — use all the students, it'll be good for them — and then I shall want you to make new parts for one horn, one trumpet and two recorders, which we have in the orchestra, out of those woodwind and brass which Haydn used but we haven't got, and please cue into Pam's cello part the timpani notes not already covered elsewhere. From half term there'll be an extra orchestra practice every week; the school is doing Bach's *Christmas Oratorio* and we are providing the orchestra — you will be conducting the preliminary rehearsals for this before Emil Spira takes it over at the end. On Thursdays you'll be going to a village west of Crediton — Bow, to carry on with the work Gerald McDonald began last year. You'll have a W.I. choir in the afternoon, a mixed orchestral class (it was indeed *very* mixed) after tea, and a choral society in the evening. Someone there will put you up for the night, and you'll be back the next morning; use the car for that, of course. Fridays are Singers' night, and we shall be starting to learn Benjamin Britten's latest choral work, *St Nicolas*, which he will conduct here next Spring. And as you may know, I am writing a book about my father's music which has to be finished over the next few months, so I shall have to rely more than usual on those of you who have already had a good musical training. (Imogen several times said to me, much later, that she'd regretted having to give this particular generation of Dartington students less of her time than others, on account of the book). But anyway, this will give you the best possible practical experience, and that's really why you came. The Music Library has plenty of material for your choirs and you will probably have to make special parts and arrangements for the Bow orchestra. I'm here to answer any questions and give any advice you need, but please give me a little warning — after lunch is usually a good time.'

She knew exactly how, and when, to push her victims in at the deep end, and she knew, also, that although they would flounder and splash about at first, it wouldn't be long before her confidence in them took over, and they would be swimming easily while she beamed approval from the bank. And Imogen would have been thrilled and delighted at the weekend gathering in celebration of her life and work, held at Dartington in September 1984, to have seen for herself how well the lessons she taught in those nine Dartington years had been assimilated, and how they are still being handed on by her students.

R.S.

Imogen in the Music Library

This is the place where a contribution would have been written by Ruth Elmhirst (Ash). Ruth gave invaluable help in the preparation for the memorial week-end, attended by so many past students, in September 1984. She was also present at the initial meeting on the project of this book.

Imogen was very fond of Ruth, encouraged her interest in singing and ensured she was involved in many choral activities. Music became an essential part of Ruth's life and something in which she actively participated until her sad, untimely death from motor neurone disease in August 1986.   *H.W.*

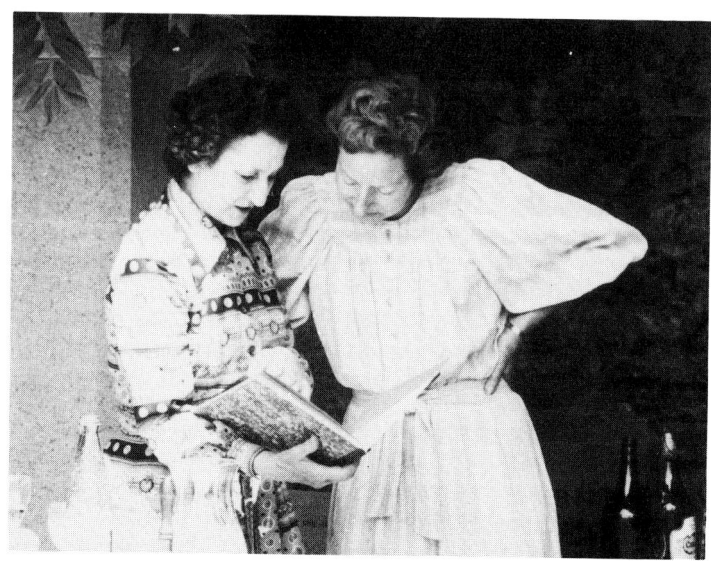

Florence Burton and Ruth Ash on the occasion of Florence's retirement

The rehearsing and performance of Bach's Mass in B Minor

The brief extracts that follow are from the many contributors who wrote of the lasting impact made by the rehearsals and performance of Bach's *Mass in B Minor*. As Imogen has already recalled in her interview with Jack Dobbs, the rehearsals extended over a period of three years. Sections of the Mass were given informal performances during that time but the main performance was on 9.7.50. *(Ed)*

DARTINGTON HALL
SUMMER FESTIVAL

In Memory of Christopher Martin

THE MASS IN B MINOR
by J. S. Bach

In commemoration of the
200th anniversary of the composer's death

Soloists:
JOAN CROSS
ROSAMUND STRODE
NOEL BARKER
ALFRED DELLER
PETER PEARS
MAURICE BEVAN
CECIL COPE

DARTINGTON SINGERS AND PLAYERS

Leader: JOSEPH SEGAL
Conductor: IMOGEN HOLST

Sunday, July 9th, 1950, at 2.30 p.m.

Imo's explanations of the marvels of Bach's harmonies remain with me to this day. *B.H.*

Imogen's performance of Bach's *B Minor Mass* has impressed my memory, as I am sure it will have impressed the minds of others who were present, as a really great occasion. The June sun shining on the Dartington gardens which had now become a rich array of many rare and colourful flowers, seemed to make the perfect setting for the coming performance. On the day before the concert, the whole of Dartington seemed to be filled with music celebrities. Benjamin Britten and Peter Pears had arrived together; they had soon been followed by Joan Cross, Anne Wood and Alfred Deller and we had the final rehearsal when the soloists were 'fitted in' to the performance as a whole. An immense amount of work had gone into this performance; Imogen had been pulling out her own score and studying various details at every possible opportunity. *J.B.*

Imogen's mental and physical energy that brought about this performance was quite remarkable. The rehearsals were special in themselves, for Imogen never showed any signs of exasperation or impatience; we just knew when she was pleased by the excitement on her face and when her footwork became more noticeable on the rostrum. She always encouraged the singers whenever possible and at the first few rehearsals the situation must have been pretty daunting, to say the least. The performance had great conviction about it, and was a real music experience for me, as I am sure it was for everyone taking part or listening to it. *E.W.*

I ought to ring round this day as one of the most profound experiences; the culmination of months of hard labour and the reward, the forging of a supple instrument that Imogen could use for the spirit that truly moved her. I have never known anything like the power of that spirit, so that we were excited or cast down to the depths. And our deepest reserves were hauled out of us — even those we did not know we possessed. *M.B.*

Her courageous rehearsals and performance of the *B Minor Mass* (which she named the greatest music in the world) involved all students and staff alike in the emotional wear and tear of detailed work and study — even the lengths of the pauses between sections were musically organised to keep the relationships in character.   K.B.

Imogen rehearsing in the Great Hall at a student reunion

Imogen as 'Student Teacher' in India: Jack Dobbs

When Imogen arrived at Dartington she found here a long established association with India, chiefly created by Leonard Elmhirst whose work in Bengal with Rabindranath Tagore had stimulated many of the ideas that were being put into practice on the Estate. India had already impinged on her own background, for her father had a deep interest in Indian philosophy, and had learnt Sanskrit in order to make as accurate a translation as possible of the passages from the Rig Veda he was setting for various combinations of voices. Unfortunately he had no opportunity to go to India himself, so when that opportunity came for Imogen, she grasped it enthusiastically, believing that the subcontinent's culture had much to offer not only to herself, but also to her Dartington students.

Her invitation to India was the direct result of something Gandhi had said to the students of Tagore's university at Santiniketan during his last visit there. Reminding them that they were members of an international university, he stressed the importance of them having a knowledge of Western music. It was to Leonard that the music staff turned to ask about the choice of teacher. There was only one answer to their question — Imogen must go. And so for the two months, December 1950 and January 1951, she was in residence at Santiniketan as a 'student-teacher' — an incredibly short time for all she hoped to achieve.

Despite her preparation from the only means available to her in England — books and gramophone records, her initial bewilderment was apparent:

"At first the sounds coming from the windows of the Santiniketan music studios were so startlingly unfamiliar that I found it difficult to write down what I was hearing, even though it was only a single line of melody. Tagore's own songs were comparatively easy to get hold of: he often borrowed traditional Bengali tunes that he had heard the boatmen singing on the river... There were also folk-songs from hill villages in the Punjab; pentatonic tunes which would have sounded equally at home in the Brendon Hills of Somerset or the Appalachian Mountains of Kentucky."

Writing home to Leonard and Dorothy Elmhirst about these Bengali songs and Punjabi dance tunes, she told them how, in turn, she was teaching both the staff and students Gregorian chants and English folk songs, adding "We have long discussions, not only about technical matters but also about teaching problems, and it is *extraordinary* to find how often the problems are *exactly* the same as ours at Dartington†".

She admitted having difficulties with the drum rhythms which at first sounded so elaborate, with their combination of exuberant freedom of invention and their strict adherence to an underlying discipline. But it was the singing technique which caused her the greatest difficulty. It took her nearly a month to get over the feeling that the singers were adding scoops in their performances to be tiresome. To her surprise, one day an Indian friend told her he thought it was a pity that European singing was so unnatural. She discovered that by this he meant the use of vibrato. This he found 'regrettable', which gave her the chance to reply that she found the scooping equally regrettable: only to realise that both of them were approaching vocal technique from within the context of their own cultural traditions;

"... I realized that it was no good wanting to exchange one for the other — it would have been just as useless as wanting to transform the hot stretch of pink sand in the banana grove into a frosty avenue of beech trees. The scooping was never an added effect. It was an essential part of what the Indians call 'expression'. And to them expression is inseparable from the shape of music; in fact the two are the same thing."

† Letter to Leonard and Dorothy Elmhirst 15.12.50.

IMOGEN AS STUDENT TEACHER IN INDIA

Her understanding of Indian singing was greatly increased when she met and heard Pandit Thakur, the Head of the Music Department at Benares University, one of the finest singers in India.

In her studies she became increasingly aware of the problems she faced teaching Western music to the Santiniketan students, for there was already a growing desire amongst the young Indian musicians to harmonize their melodies and orchestrate their tunes in a Western manner, with little to guide them but film music. She felt strongly that if Indians wanted to harmonize their music they would have to discover how to do it themselves, and not rely on ready made imports from the West. One specific influence from the West which she felt so passionately about as to call 'pernicious' was the small hand-harmonium which had been introduced in the nineteenth century, and which she believed was destroying the indigenous concepts of pitch and interval.

Although she enjoyed her stay in Santiniketan immensely, and waxed lyrical about it in her letters back to Dartington there were times when she felt worried about the future for Indian music. Often she was asked by the young writers, painters and architects she met in Calcutta, "But is there a future for Indian Music? Surely it has come to a dead end, hasn't it?".

I hope Imogen would be re-assured by the way the fine musicians who have come to Dartington to perform and teach since her time here have brought with them the finest elements of their music — with no compromise — and have proved that it remains very much alive. She was pleased when Indian music became an integral part of all the music courses at the College, and I think she would have been happy with the latest developments — the establishment of a tabla training course where both Indian and European students work together to learn and pass on the art which she so much respected.

Her notes giving her reasons for wanting to study Indian music before she went to Santiniketan contain the illuminating sentence "We are at last beginning to learn about music outside Europe". That was in 1950. We have moved quite a long way since then, and to that progress Imogen and her visit to India made a valuable contribution.

It was typical of Imogen that she should thank Dorothy and Leonard Elmhirst for all that Dartington had given her. We, who were fortunate enough to be her students, also know what an extra dimension has been added to our lives through being at Dartington and experiencing the inspiration of Imogen's teaching.

> August 6th, 1947.
>
> Dearest Leonard and Dorothy,
>
> I wanted to try and say thank you for the loveliest year I've ever known, but it's difficult to know where to begin. It has been so very much the best year I've yet had for teaching, as well as for learning about music. It's not just that I've been very, very lucky with my twenty-one students. And it's not just that it gets easier to learn as one gets older. But it's much more that Dartington itself grows on one all the time. When I first came I thought of it as a fascinating but difficult job that was waiting to be done, and I reckoned that its beauty and its freedom and the luxury would be drawbacks rather than assets, and that one would have to put in a lot of hard work in order to create anything real. But now after five years of it I see how hopelessly wrong I was, and I realise that it is Dartington itself that does everything and that teaches one everything. And that far from putting anything in, we just take what we want all the time, and thrive on it.
>
> Thank you for everything.
>
> All my love,
> Imogen.

As with so many occasions at Dartington, it would be appropriate to end this personal tribute to Imo by a round, written by one of her early students, Edith O'Hanrahan.

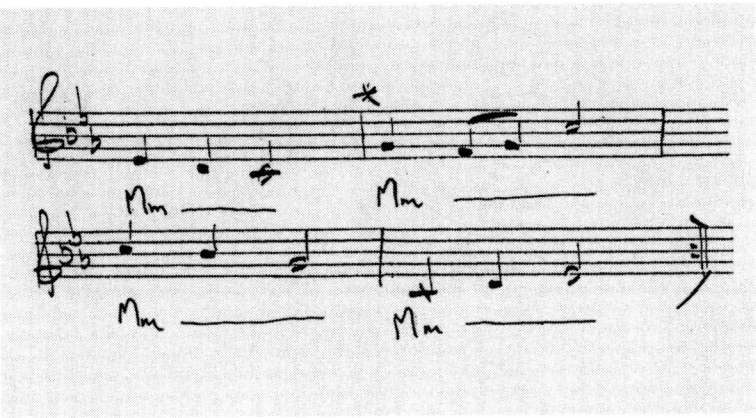